CRACKER SONNETS

CRACKER SONNETS

Poems by Amy Wright

BRICK ROAD
POETRY PRESS

Cover art: "Bird Train" painting © Sheep Jones

Author photo: Don Sudbrink

Library of Congress Control Number: 2016941376
ISBN-13: 978-0-9898724-8-5

Published by Brick Road Poetry Press
P. O. Box 751
Columbus, GA 31902-0751
www.brickroadpoetrypress.com

Brick Road logo by Dwight New

*For my parents,
who have an ongoing debate
about whether Zesta or Premium
makes the best saltine.*

Acknowledgments

Special thanks to Kristy Bowen of Dancing Girl Press who published a selection of these poems in the chapbook *Cracker Crumbs in the Bed, Rhinestones.*

Thanks as well to the editors of the following journals in which earlier versions of these poems appeared: *2River, American Letters & Commentary,* Architrave Press, Edition 3, *ArLiJo, Bluestem, Burlesque Press Variety Show, Hard Lines: Rough South Poetry* anthology, *Ibbetson Street, The Labletter, Newfound,* and *Quarterly West.*

Thanks also to Tom Daley, Mary Kennedy Brown, Jamie Duncan, Jesse Graves, David Huddle, Charlotte Pence, Amy Pickworth, and all the other Holy Mackerels who contributed their apple-pie-rollers, Lester Flatt kinfolk, and one-handed fiddlers to this cast of characters.

Contents

I.

I.

Jax Ovie Blows Perfect Smoke Rings in Farnham's Musty Playhouse

Morning throttles Jax's motor,

lowers her frost skirt for him,

if someone else's bride. *Let Lambs*

work their way up class ladders

with Starter hats and Nikes, he

thinks when Colleen clicks past

ignoring catcalls, heels snapping concrete,

a jar of maraschino cherries jiggling, ready

to be tossed into her Alka-Seltzer

before she drops wasp-waisted onto the

stage apron, owing nothing to no man

and off all day tomorrow.

Daughertys Don't Live like Whitfields

with ponytails
tucked under trucker caps, clambering
up fig boughs rapt by Kentucky racetracks'
orphic buzz,
but like migratory Arctic terns
who top Tew Knob and yodel out of earshot,
voices joyriding peaks and valleys.

No blue kite ducks their cottonwoods
only to nosedive tomato vines. No stuck
drawer is their laughter, whittled
albatross their suggestion box.

Blessed addicts with 24-hour drugstore panacea,
they sigh in recliners, lungs a euphonic accordion,
steady, fathomable, and absolute.

Eye of Every Storm

Fat Ehud sips ash, one knee cocked
on rusted bumpers, jabs elbows down Central
High hallways, bowls Star Williams into
lockers, unlit cigarette dribbling
scorn, denim jacket thrown
down with aplomb.
Motorcyle idling, prepped
to litter night's oceanic pastures,
fingers snapping like pinged gravel
so that nothing about that town is the same
come morning, thirst's slick stone
in a bedside Dixie cup, white crickets
nibbling horizon's goblin rind.

Virginia Leabus' Dreams Are Stuffed Chicken Wire Parading Promises

After two failed marriages, Virginia goes on
sauerkraut diets, splits hogsheads of molasses
with Martha, shreds deeds. Her ribs
bowed pines under snow, her eyes flyspecked
windows in bright sun.
She hangs upturned bells and horseshoe talismans
of hope she may live beyond the life she was given,
pulls two beers clinking from the refrigerator,
a sleeve of light flaring in her dark apartment.

"What it means to have a woman's body,"
she tells her daughter, "is to stand at the mouth of the cave
and be the cave. Bats flying out of it like hearts."

Coralee Robbins Showers in the Dark

in clawfoot bathtubs, coos bless yous, raising
heron-blue fishermen with waved handkerchiefs.
Harried, she rear-ends a Civic on Jefferson,
drawls, bottom lip a curl of baler twine,
forgets to mind her dead, circles lakes and bonfires,
howls over slick-glazed, sweet-sauced carcasses,
which she fingertip-dabs with Wetnaps,
communing foremost with the holy
mackerels of deliciousness.

Bea Lineberry Doesn't Deserve This.
What Does It Mean to Deserve.

Bea renders the Beloved's fat into Crisco,
pours her heart into the great collaborative
dumbwaiter, consoles herself with peppermint
toddies & Hershey's syrup, toe trails sunset-pecked
barns' slow fade, dreams in third person, gorges
mahogany bookcases with series romances, fasts
after backwoods church services until nothing
is ordinary or all things are.

Convoys Nucleate in Pizza Hut Parking Lots like Blue Angel Formations at an Air Show

Roy and Lynn play games like Barbara Is Electric

and I Am A Radio Song, Rumble in the Nurses'

Station, and Beg. They launder hands on mango-colored

hand towels after fixing the car. Always fixing

cars or produce stands or each other, so many Adcocks

have their windows tinted they have nearly conquered

happiness in the form of license plate identification,

which they frame in purple lights to find "Hankstr" and

"Lalabrd" and "Pandoo" across Vesuvian arrow-streaked

plains. They turn forty-five without Benedictine

in their cupboards, likening all such collectibles

to lint cakes one eventually learns to dispense with.

Ann Christian Wouldn't Be Caught Dead Baking Cornpone

When Ann was six years old, the Easter
Bunny didn't come
until Mother got up, which made her wise.
Later, petals stuck to her forehead
after a rain, making her appear gentle
like someone falling asleep under a tanning bed,
which made her brave
since looks can be deceiving.

Good grades in high school
status-elevated her parents, unsuspecting
her after-honors-club education
watching Coach Movell and Mrs. Juarez
in the gym room with the lights off.

Thirty-something, she flutters
from wing-tipped offices, nails manicured
peach slices, frosted eyes daring
the unavoidable argument to start living
again and again in each moment.

Twelve J.V. Cheerleaders on a Bus
Encounter a Band of Aliens

Thanks to local d.j., Danny G, a nubile team
gathers to be filmed for a believe-it-or-not
show on alien sightings, although the girls
have not themselves spotted extra terrestrials.
They don candybar-sales-bought short skirts,
lips glossed Too Faced and Sugared Apricot.

When the camera rolls, they point wide-eyed
from schoolbus windows in a daylit parking lot—
at nothing. Between takes, they laugh and crack
cookies whose fortunes assure them
everyone will come to their birthday pool parties.
Stationed by the windows, they prepare
unbelievably trustworthy faces, gazes lifted
to supposed crafts' coming. It's ghostly,
how you can almost see squadrons before them
like pretty gunshot.

Marge Piloh Needs to Do Her Multiplication Homework *before* She Gets Pregnant Next Time

Better mission to Africa than trailer houses

saving souls who stand in living argument

to Father Hand's word, offer nothing but

unbearable neighbor likenesses. Marge browns

to almond and marries Tumelo—threads intermingling

patterns like fishermen's wives knitted homing devices

into their sweaters, so no matter where she goes,

someone can tell her "Cracker, you are from Nebraska,"

only in their coexistent language, which is spitten.

If We Love Not Each Other, How Can We Love Gigi Whom We Have Not Seen?

"Money is no foremost matter,"

read forgotten flea-market journals—

"but that split fish multiplied to feed thousands,

proliferating like transplanted grass

carp in the Choctawhatchee River."

Loose stuck pages and you will have not one

but a consort of experts parked in the road

talking sideways through driver-side windows,

saying you know, only you know where to go next.

One Pot

of wienies redder, saltier than the other
Alma Pristridge brought to the fellowship
barbecue. Owl-shawled, she paces the churchyard
Gatorade trucks barrel past after second shift
to fertilize Dowd's bluestem with its nitrogen
runoff, smiles at demure Boos who wait
while others grab thickest-iced cupcakes,
sweeps as the wind sweeps, without expecting
thanks. Beneath the porch swing, mutts sleep
after killing sheep with mountain neighbors
in fits of neither greed nor mercy,
though a pure bred Labrador is put down for it.

Off-brand Paper Towels Sop Up the Ever-loving Bounty

Bevode McCall spit-turns an annual summer pig

in beer marinade and calls in the Floyd

County Reed brothers to dobro fingerpick.

Previous party-goers lavish praise Tim Crockett

publishes in the weekend insert Bevode flips past

along with Silver Queen's going rate. Cedar-scented

Stella reels to their genius stringwork, taunts

onlooking Odom who thinks her one twig shy

of a nest to act so uninhibited, but she just downcasts

her eyes while Paul and Stevie mend between their

fingertips the delicate furious.

II.

Best Soapbox's Full of Soap

Edna Vaughn says too much is said
while our bodies are strung up & twanged,
bent grasses beside a time-riven pier
drawn apart by slick hooks of river, pitted
by cramped quarters' piercing stares. She
feeds seven children Vienna sausages, patches
roofs of clapboard houses, sets out alloy silverware
like cavalry, says, "To be forgotten is to be true.
In spite of everything, there is perfect refuge
in heart's dark spotless town."

"In Juno, They Got Northern Lights, But Betelgeuse and Cassiopeia Come Every Summer to Franklin Park."

July creek nights, lightning bugs star sycamores

for the ten o'clock showing of Nikki's hot pink brassiere strap

and Grady's Ready-lite dynamite—the original firecrackers,

eyes dusted with lemon-yellow-tailpipe reflections

while 2,000 miles away a young New Zealander points to the

      Aurora

Borealis and asks his father, "How did all the rainbows get drunk?"

which the ex-pat, who still has feelings for his first wife, answers,

dancing the product of their union in a shamrock pattern, "On the

rye whiskey lemonade of Agenbite's Inwit, my sweet chaser!"

Leda Burk Crosses Herself

to pay respect to passing hearses, saves pajamas

for hospital stays. When a Cascade-dish-detergent baron

winds carnival necklaces around her daughter's gear shift,

proposes by twining tinsel around her wedding finger,

they air out the parlor, dotted with tin cans and Gaelic

spears, plunge giddy into rabbit-fur-packed armoires,

knowing, even before he vanishes months on end,

reappears with a gallows branch, the remains will be

transparent and the guards ill-timed.

Ironically, Brocade Bedclothes of Rain
Reduce the Quantity of All Potable Water

After a flash flood, car washes close
to conserve drinking water. "Do you
think I'm weird?" Joe Junior asks a
stranger, staring at houses up to their
windows in brackish water. His excitement
shames him; he cusses, puts his hat on
backwards to mask it. She smiles, gentle
as mailbox tongues lapping like paddles.
"No," she tells him, thinking, *innocent.*

Sunday Afternoon Apocalypse

There's nothing left
but Composition teachers and Bic pens.
Helios' horses doze in their stables
like hounds post hunt. A bunch of soaks
roll on moss drying out. Boone Cranddock
and C.D. Bowdoin hang ten toes off a pickup tailgate,
disinherited viceroys positioned to reclaim
kaput heathland, high school flashes in the pan,
steroidy starlings that won't go out.

Edna Culpepper Buries Her Hound Dog with Shovelsful of Verbiage

Scored earth, muddy with rainwater,

coughs up Ricola wrappers. Edna ambles

barefoot past natural-pharmaceuticals-

lined driveways. A jeepful of teenagers honk,

lifting Blue Ribbons as if at an awards ceremony.

Due to a buzzard kettle overhead,

letter carriers listen when elders ask them

not to bring any more bills.

"Aw, to Hell with Recreation, Let's Just Survive," Willow Scratches on Ziploc Baggies

Desire will hang you out to dry, Willow
tells her sorority, "over a canyon,
with no one to cut you down or hear
you howl. I'm not going to be one of them
who will lie to you. The weapons you need
are inside. Polish until they shine. Your
reflection may stop you. Be interested in it,
as you would a small and toothy mammal
chewing grass. Be disinterested in it,
as you would a long-standing tie.
Wear your pin. Share the experience with
your sisters. A needle is a tiny determinant
knife."

Belle Neely Quit Listening to Aunt Mildred

Braving plaid in the thigh area, Belle spits
watermelon seeds into the sideyard.
No one had to say so. She can see for herself
brick masons laying pug for the patio, diners
wielding chopsticks, her grandfather massaging
mink oil into leather. She watched Rheese
extract meth chutes from insoles, the Brisons
scramble to county lockup where planning
dawns on her as useless, if time equals money
and money can't buy happiness.

John-John's Unavailable

to bring ginger ale to Avery feverish
on the sofa, nailing that Styx
riff on his Stratocaster. *Tough break,*
but she hardscrabbles over it, knuckle-dusts
daisy pillows into the headboard grunting,
while the tendony roughneck trims trees
shirtless, tan as outlaws, tough as jerky.
She chews ice, kicks lint,
until he mewls from the bedroom so longingly
he seems to have been there always.

Jubilee, Methodist Basement Every Sunday

Scarlett Marett stopped drinking milk

to clear her sinuses, indebting cattle,

since every reduced teaspoon eases

masticated udders. Although

no one on the river rafting cares really,

she *is* dazzling, warbling

like gargled pebbles. Oblivious

children throw frisbee, every one of them

filled with more potential than a DC motor.

She invites them over—if only

they will start afresh, baby teeth

white as blank pages, original

innards clean as arrows.

Flycatchers in the Sorrel Patch

Robin cartwheels over sourwood-bronzed grass.
"The only kind of honey we've had
to pour out," her mother says, disapproving
of waste and mascara on daughters
before age thirteen. Penny chews
raspberry balm off her lip, which reflects
in the aluminum scrap pile like a pink zirconia
ring Greg slid onto her cousin Tammy.
Luellen sticks her finger in the jar and swirls,
pulling out a strand like Christmas taffy.
"Tastes sweet to me," she says, licking
her siren-shell nail clean. Stringy hired hands
eye the girls like field mice from the barn roof,
tin-colored sealant glistening in their trays
like wolf pelts. Janene tugs her tanktop strap,
runs a finger along the jar's mouth, shining
her lips. "You expect to finish in time
to go to the fair painting like that?" she trills,
startling a meadowlark off the fencepost
where his uplifted throat was resounding
a case for himself.

Ruby Woodard Learns Something New Every Day

Sifting misinformation keeps Ruby humble. If it were dirt,

she could plant tomatoes, but it is powder. It is flour, sugar.

Violet dips fingers in and crosses her, saying "You are dusted!

You are ashen! You are invisible!" It layers her.

Later Emma blows it off softly, "Lover!" she calls her, grateful.

III.

Note on the Back of a Photograph
from Ida Rudd to Abraham Cochran

Pilled wool

of frost on the transom

& me too short of breath to O

a pane of glass or cuss

the Council president

of Progress Park who let this house

decay for want

of maintenance, *Dryopteris*

marginalis (Leather Woodfern)

reclaiming the flooded basement.

Trade Times Advertisement

Hazel Sikes' jewelweed tincture
for poison ivy
is better than calamine lotion.

Of course, her number's
unlisted.

As if Unchanged for Centuries

Wooden-tined hay rake

in the tool shed propped

against the icebox where blackberry

tea sweats treefrog

eyeball-sized globules.

Piney Donegan Fell in the Feed Trough

Tripped on slick grass

in blind reverie,

narrow burrow in the mammal

sheets of the seductress, Ada Myall,

with her giant nipple—a pocked thimble

in her breast pocket, handleless bucket, fire

without a candle.

"I Am What I Want to Be," Shreve

tells the police detective who says,
You're clever enough to be anything,
after they haul his mop back to Big Sandy,
having escaped his ninth penitentiary.
He works acrostics in the library, ruminates
his spit, undoes Joy Ellen with the way he walks—
boot laces whip, heels planting with each step
like any minute he's about to turn around.

Shots of Communion

rain quaff Sand Mountain.
Water grows cress, stinging
nettles strangle, poke
passes ankles, poisons.

The Farmhand

Shirttail cascading

like cloven hooves

trampling a mountain aflame

with drought,

the man in the would-be grass

walks—a bag of nickels being dropped

atop a spring-loaded shotgun—

speaks so rarely he might be a colloidal

plate awaiting an imprint

of a hundred thrushes

exiting a lake

named for the seldom-seen

swan.

A Good Quandary

Brushed by a smoke fox
of wiregrass
agrime with noon
sun, Boo hums—a sawbuzz
bumblebee, the plait of her
voice two boards crossed
over a barred window
widowed from the road,
high-ceiling chimneys charged with sonar.
Fill this pine-abutted soundscape
with song, or listen?
Under the gutter
cochleae of fiddlehead ferns
await rain.

Distinguishing Species

The first vertebrate begat another vertebrate that developed lungs, begat another vertebrate that over millions of years begat spider monkeys, who couldn't have stopped if they wanted to before begetting Niamh who begat Keeva who almost begat Ciara but begat Miss USA, Sophie McCalister Baker, who begat half of Springfield with the midwivery assistance of Caireanne, Ida, Romy, and brown-eyed Caitlin from Bransom County, among nameless others thanks to raspberry leaf, shepherds purse, comfrey, crampbark, blue cohosh, motherwort, uva ursi, and witch hazel, in the undiscriminating company of apple aphids, velvet worms, ladybirds, midges, gall wasps, leafhoppers, woollybears, and bean thrips, who help make the planet habitable for a God-given range of muskrats, mastiffs, ocelots, cinnamon bears, and yellow-pine chipmunks, who exhibit such characteristics as single lower jaw bones that attach to the skull, deciduous teeth, expandable and non-expanding cheeks and other pouch options, modified sweat glands, two atria and ventricles, the ability to regulate body temperature, varying in mating rituals, reproductive numbers, and social networking dos and don'ts otherwise known as culture.

In That Place

To paint one rose equals a life in that place.

—Fanny Howe

I

Backhoe operator shaves
a beard of snow with a bucket razor.
The one of several
state employees who leaves
the cleanest neckline, trims
hoary hairs in a cleft chin,
misses nothing—no grizzled dimple,
icy washboard. A tender develops
tenderness for the land, his jackdaw body
singing in the cab.
When a plot comes up for sale,
he purchases it, pulls an articulated arm
through the dirt, breaking ground. Looks inside
her hills.

II

The Cambrian Earth
populated the ocean
with a sophisticated visual system
of some fifteen thousand lenses
in a single eye. Trilobites saw depth of field
through stone, calcite inner cells of their scopes
visible in a CT scan—magnified—a diamond-
shaped photorecepter surrounded by petals,
a fossilized flower before the terrestrial world
evolved flowers. For over 270 million years
they proliferated, eye stalks to see above
mud, shades for light-dappled
trawlers. A long love
doing with the sea what sex does,
antennae diddling the floor.

III

A radiologist scrutinizes internal
borders on silver-impregnated films,
is paid handsomely for differentiating
pre-invasive lesions from ground-glass
nodules, lives on the same dirt
road as the backhoe operator,
throws up a hand when they pass door
to handled door, eyes in the same meeting place
on their faces.

IV

Horsetail lines the neighborhood
stream, living fossil, the only remaining member
of the genus *Equisetum*. Silicates on bristles,
scouring rush for tin cups, the understory of Paleozoic
forests. Their moisture-sensitive springs
disperse spores instead of seed
when the sack splits like a hose full of silt
half-buried in the garden
duct tape raveling around its toffee
mouth.

V

Blighted chesnuts
recover on suburban lawns.
Sheep's legs taper
pencil point wicks
in the cool tallow of alfalfa,
blood moon nails
over an oil pan.

IV.

Yards Clapped with Geese

Nothing to do
until fog lifts

over the cornfield. Someone pinches spearmint
leaves around tobacco,

tosses dandelion greens
with red clover. Saucered

coffee cools. Buses clack
past shouldered with workers, isolation

at such times untraversable,
though some of the women exchange thermoses,

sandwiches, guffaw at cemeteries,
study each other's inscrutable manners.

Daw Kegley installs hinges
while Claire's thumb grows misshapen.

A number straddle
appareled horses.

Tracking devices crow

from orchard to vineyard, tags

bearing the economic motto,

"Only God lives forever."

Being Jed Duman is like getting a degree in knowing better

than to count on anybody. After Joe Bryant accidentally waved

him into oncoming traffic, he one-upped his weight-room buddy,

t-shirt boasting: "School of Hard Knocks and Late Answers,"

his defensive logic circular, the way the baddest Atticus

on the playground smacked his mother for scrubbing mustard

off his cheek and rolled his eyes to heaven, ashamed of her.

You make your own fortune, Rhett snickers, sitting by interstate
-median pignuts. Leaves submit like ledgers on which old accounts
are being settled. Bark frays his paintbrush.

Smudge-faced children mimic him dabbling each flame-
colored bubble. He admonishes the curious little salamanders
who get paint in their eyes and bawl, hiccupping like drunkards.

Amabel and James just want Pop to like them. But
he looks abashed. Maybe he can't explain it, or maybe
he doesn't like them as much as he thought when they first had
     them.

Nobody plays in firehydrant fountains but Tegs Turpin.

If she wants to go to Paris, Tennessee last minute, she calls a cousin

to cover her shift and hops on Dunk Johnson's motorcycle.

They're invisible

when envious policemen set their lights rolling.

"Eeeerraaaaaoowwwg!"

Ferocious with gawdawful demons, they gobble circus peanuts

and peanut brittle and glamorously skinny cigarettes,

canceling input with Japanese headphones.

For awhile no one can hear anybody else. "Uyhuuunnnnnbbbb,"

coppers babble. Tegs pretends to have beach front property,

sells it, moves to Lincoln, to Omaha, to Normal.

She can be happy anywhere. When things don't go her way,

anything weaker than an NSR500 can do it without her.

We'll never get it,

Grainger admits to Nahuel, laughing.

They slap each other's backs, in route

to shotgun houses where no one awaits them,

bare-knuckled, scabby with data.

Guzzling lager, Hawk spills from oriel windows.
Stray dog ambulances cry down the road:
"oooOOOOOOOOOnnnnnoorrrrrrnnnnnAAAAh!"

Jimbo smokes Pam's last two Luckies. Unnoticed,
fifteen-year-old Nikki pulls knees to chest in the desert-rose
recliner where she woke in Nay-nay's called-back lap

when she was seven. Muttonchop comes home from third shift,
flings himself onto the sofa where knotted bodies squirm, molt
of captive wings peeling like sunburned skin without freeing them.

"Boring!" youngsters proclaim at the family reunion
while adults yak about real estate. They take action
and tackle each other for paper footballs.
"Listen," fathers coach, "you might learn something."
No chance, they think. We don't want to end up like you anyway.
Brought home to a country modular with Janene to homeschool
him, Dirk might be anything, logrolling down hills on which bow
and shrug poppies. A snail shell on the woodpile catches his eye
as if it crawled all the way here from the ocean that rose up
a billion years ago and receded, eroding the Appalachians,
though he still can't believe it.

V.

Clove to the Rock of the Spirit

There's always something
to watch—old men on trailer porches

scan traffic, teenagers,
in mothers' company, censor

bit phrases, little girls scout
airborne pans, dodge

punches mum
as bug-eyed mice caught in mousetraps.

Sometimes no one even notices
they see it all from the back seat

clear as Windex—
Sue's jealous husband

who locks her in evenings,
Georgia's pom-squad uniform

grown tight in the belly, Roger praying
for the Second Coming:

"Lord help us, God almighty,"
which said in vain might be cussing.

But the Holy Spirit comes
to him.

He gets a faroff look listening,
ear cocked as if to a train

or a woman coming around,
and his lips part a sly corner.

The Family Tree Swings

Vic Blunt doesn't want to leave home's creature comforts

daughter Sylvie learns on a trip to California

where tannins' subtle breathing wastes on him, whose

wine preference leans toward homemade strawberry.

"Tastes like ink!" he complains. It is just a matter of

education, Sylvie knows and gets hers

being observant. Truckers wink knowingly while she studies

their signals, throwing orange skins out the window

where they spiral like letters written in a very foreign language.

Sweet Cheeks Calls Dragonflies Snake Doctors and Weddings off at Sometimes the Last Minute

Same as there are waffling politicians and fence-sitting voters,

Dolores gabs about moving to Michigan, somewhere

easier to raise twin girls than airconditionless houses where

pollen coats the mantle and doily weavers crawl in your

hip boots. But in Ann Arbor, elevators gum up, Lansing's

Commissioner mismanages revenue, and the world over

metes out the same chopped pork, only worse

because unfamiliar, which is how she convinces herself

to stay put and, awhile anyway, single.

Schoolbus House

When Hud and Beth moved
into the schoolbus, it was easier
than walking back to town, until winter,
when they argued loud and often
about Hud's drinking, stray cats Beth fed,
how unnecessary it is to want things
to be different.

Hud milked the Holsteins.
Beth sharpened the axe handle with a bastard file,
stretched a chicken's neck with a length,
brought down the blade—
that chicken never taking its eyes away
from the string, fool neck outstretched toward it.

Source of All Things

If Norlene needs a garden trowel
or porcelain sink stand

or bug spray or length of chain
to bolt the gate, it is in the outbuilding

somewhere. It might need to be rejiggered
like the lawnmower pull cord,

otherwise fashioned
like the apple butter cauldron in the front yard

full of hens-and-biddies,
but there is rarely a need

to drive to town for it.
She robs Peter to pay Paul

and brings them both a box of catch-alls
next yard sale.

Lloyd too never throws away a remnant
walnut slice after joining a table

he might use for picture frames
or drawer pulls.

If he hadn't saved that cherry bedpost,
who knows

when he wouldn've gotten around to
carving Walton that potato masher,

since he wouldn't any more waste
virgin wood on a little job

than slaughter a pig
for the jowls.

Of course once the animal is killed,
it's only right to use every part

but the squeal, Norlene says,
having known hunger's almighty finger

to scoop a hollow in her
belly, make her swear

disasters are questions of willingness
to act and to be answered.

The Burnetts Are What They Make

Jayne shovels dirt
        cake onto the kids' plates.

Becca blends handsoap with downy brome
        and milk thistle.

J.D. converts his front yard into a quail sanctuary
        and Reed does 360s in the mudlot

behind the nylons factory. Arn and Desi
        devote one room in their Victorian

to Robert Louis Stevenson and another to
        Mona Lisa.

Loretta (a.k.a. Dancing Bear) bakes seven-banana
        banana bread,

which creates trouble when she operates her concessions
        stand sans permit. Neighbors call the police

when Amy Lou fires a hole into the Hoosier,
        J.J. puts sugar in Jesús's gas tank,

Arlan paints the Dickson Subway

    chartreuse with blue moonlight,

which gets his chain status revoked,

    but he can't care about that now, being an artist.

One Word after Another Word Is Unclean

Rev. Mabe preaches that the throat is an open grave,
borrowing Paul's phrase, to lash cautelous tongues,
though he'd not say so if he too were not condemned
by baser nature, willing to commit ignoble acts if no one's wiser.

Terry Lee keeps Esther's bone-baring secrets,
who keeps Winslow's, who keeps Rose's,
who keeps Brother Preston's, who thanks everyone for coming
to church this morning, fresh as he is from the hospital
to sing how the Lord will lead them to higher ground.

Macon romanticizes houses with syrup-giving maples,
plays the lottery but chances his aleatoric future to nothing
except the Ten Commandments and eternal damnation
or reward that awaits him, the final decision uncertain,
since he doesn't follow the Decalogue like Sister Linda.

Devil Dogs wear black anklets with flip-flops,
affix cattle horns to Cadillac hoods.
Arn won't buy more clothes than he has chrome hangers.
Manny carries every bathtub spider out in a Solo cup.
Truck won't desecrate his flesh unless
the tattoo means something, and Helen wears only blue eyeliner.

"But not even one congregant is good in their hearts,"
the Reverend says, "though the great gift of Grace is that God
forgives them," piled into the sanctuary after sermon,
buzzards into ravens, eating Isabelle's peach cobbler.

Blood Bath Baby

Children allowed to be
children in high chairs—spoons
overhead like Puritan-forest torches,
misfits, woodwose, Jezebels—yawp
for MORE! beet mush
even as it covers feedbag,
forehead, keyring-size
footprints. Little do they know
messy cleronomy will soon
splotch lily-white faces,
blueberry-wine stain
four-chambered-chalice
altarcloths. As soon as they
start their periods, take Communion,
park in the Lover's Lane cul-de-sac,
it will all be over—whatever
kept them from becoming
yellow dogs and bigots, no-count
leaches fattened on government's tick
hounds. Regional typecasts
skinny-dipping snapping turtles'
gene pool, tongues twisted
around eye teeth so they can't see
what they're saying.

Grandfather's grandfather's
great-uncle was a bastard
unmentioned in county annals.
Great-aunt Mary Margaret
shot her husband on the toilet
with her lady pistol.
So many land-poor cousins
or dyspeptics were locked up,
put away, or shut themselves in
some squatters' cabin.
Deacon forgot where they put
the family Bible detailing
patrimony customs for drawing off
one's sandal only to throw it in
the river of true riches, Granny's fried-pie
recipe for apples that did not fall far
from the tree. But that crime
scene moment in the kitchen,
brilliant with vermilion—
they are citizens of no country
but babyhood, not yet Redskins or
Patriots, fans of no team
but a planet that produces pearlescent
onions with snow peas, cherry
tomatoes and non-chlorine bleach.

The Feuding Pruitts

Marge detested Hal's taste in pickups and glared at his
airbrushed t-shirt as if the lance of her
disapproval fit the Divine Judge's chamber keyhole. Sol
poisoned Manny's whole herd unknowingly planting yew
trees by the pasture. Adelaide's hair caught fire while she
was frying chicken, and Gretchen's sides split laughing.
Then her baby was born without a pelvis, George Richard
shot his face off trying to right the fallen gun in the cabinet,
and Billy drowned when his family went on vacation. After that,
all their vitriol faded, eased up like a gum-sore alligator
on a flank steak, and they sat together watching bluegill
school as if there were profit in it.

Gadfreys Challenge Pentecost Values

Ava saw a family riven by liquor sober,

her grandfather preach out a string

of venom, hammered

on the prophets' word, called

to leave carpentry, swap his father's brew

for one that never—even when money runs out—

stops flowing, the podium skinned

of its worldly varnish. A dozen incomprehensible

tongues licking the body's vents.

His wife allowed herself to be taken

over by the   *Yes, yes*

Lord to that realm which surpasseth

understanding. Ava's love

for her the color of locusts.

She left them

the way grandfather's father would go

on a month-long drunk, piss the bed,

spend every red cent of grocery money.

Eyes flickered distant, arms raised away from her.

Then, they came back.

                              He even stayed years
                              without touching a drop.
Fire receded
to a blue glint and she'd make beans and biscuits.

Habitat

Mac and Paulie cling to the mountainside,
sphagnum moss on an abalone camper.

Their father collects disability.
They are ingenious

manipulators of flag girls
in parking lots, track stars in waffle-joint

back booths, french fryers in ferris wheel
top buckets,

at home unable to avoid
introducing them to Pudding

on the sofa, their young mother
who makes them pretend she's their sister.

Mud puppies
cut through a school of crappies,

patch the shallows, sprout
toes sensitive as tentacles

on a slug's head—
ascend the muck thin-skinned

as newborns, or did back then.
Of course, Mac will grow up,

start a tree-trimming business,
meet Scottie who isn't afraid

of his wolf pup or long silences,
how a hard storm closes

their exit. Imperiled
water shrews and hellbender

playthings give her something to lose
in that nothing-much mobile—

a freshwater turtle
she feeds periodically

a handful of cereal that crackles
when wet like maggots.

Do you want to move someplace else?
Mac asks after lovemaking, her nape wet,

fan blades slowing with her pulse.
Eddie has a body shop in Lafayette. . . .

Scottie pulls a squirrel's tail
curl through a hairbrush

she keeps near the bed, like all Peary women.
Away from here I wouldn't know

what it looks like to be happy,
she says. I would test it

the way a girl will suffer her love
to prove his love real,

wouldn't hear the mourning dove
or see the Blazing Star

nod its fandango assent from a far
field. No, it is better to know chorus frogs

are in danger, the lake sturgeon
almost lost.

What are those creatures to me
I cannot be sorry never to have seen?

About the Author

Amy Wright's collection *Cracker Sonnets* was a finalist for the Brick Road Poetry Prize. Her debut poetry collection, *Everything in the Universe*, was published by Iris Press. Nonfiction Editor of Zone 3 Press, Associate Professor, and Coordinator of Creative Writing at Austin Peay State University, her work has been published in *Kenyon Review, Hard Lines: Rough South Poetry*, and *Southern Poetry Anthology* (Volumes III and VI), and five chapbooks. Together with William Wright she co-authored *Creeks of the Upper South*. She has received a Peter Taylor Fellowship for the Kenyon Review Writers' Workshop and Individual Artist's Fellowship from the Tennessee Arts Commission. Some of her writing is online at www.awrightawright.com.

Our Mission

The mission of Brick Road Poetry Press is to publish and promote poetry that entertains, amuses, edifies, and surprises a wide audience of appreciative readers. We are not qualified to judge who deserves to be published, so we concentrate on publishing what we enjoy. Our preference is for poetry geared toward dramatizing the human experience in language rich with sensory image and metaphor, recognizing that poetry can be, at one and the same time, both familiar as the perspiration of daily labor and as outrageous as a carnival sideshow.

Also Available from Brick Road Poetry Press

www.brickroadpoetrypress.com

Bad Behavior by Michael Steffen

Tracing the Lines by Susanna Lang

Rising to the Rim by Carol Tyx

Treading Water with God by Veronica Badowski

Rich Man's Son by Ron Self

Just Drive by Robert Cooperman

The Alp at the End of My Street by Gary Leising

The Word in Edgewise by Sean M. Conrey

Household Inventory by Connie Jordan Green

A Meal Like That by Albert Garcia

Practice by Richard M. Berlin

Battle Sleep by Shannon Tate Jonas

Things Seen by Joseph Stanton

Also Available from Brick Road Poetry Press
www.brickroadpoetrypress.com

Dancing on the Rim by Clela Reed

Possible Crocodiles by Barry Marks

Pain Diary by Joseph D. Reich

Otherness by M. Ayodele Heath

Drunken Robins by David Oates

Damnatio Memoriae by Michael Meyerhofer

Lotus Buffet by Rupert Fike

The Melancholy MBA by Richard Donnelly

Two-Star General by Grey Held

Chosen by Toni Thomas

Etch and Blur by Jamie Thomas

Water-Rites by Ann E. Michael

About the Prize

The Brick Road Poetry Prize, established in 2010, is awarded annually for the best book-length poetry manuscript. Entries are accepted August 1st through November 1st. The winner receives $1000 and publication. For details on our preferences and the complete submission guidelines, please visit our website at www.brickroadpoetrypress.com.